What Are Literatur

In *Literature Pockets—Folktales and Fairy Tales*, eight familiar stories come alive through fun, exciting projects. The activities for each story are stored in a labeled pocket made from construction paper. (See directions below.) Add the charming cover and fasten the pockets together to make a personalized Folktales and Fairy Tales book for each student to enjoy.

How to Make the Pockets

1. Use a 12″ x 18″ (30.5 x 45.5 cm) piece of construction paper for each pocket. Fold up 6″ (15 cm) to make a 12″ (30.5 cm) square.
2. Staple the right side of the pocket closed.
3. Punch two or three holes in the left side of the pocket.

How to Make the Cover

1. Reproduce the cover illustration on page 3 for each student.
2. Have students color and cut out the illustration and glue it onto a 12″ (30.5 cm) square piece of construction paper to make the cover.
3. Punch two or three holes in the left side of the cover.
4. Fasten the cover and the pockets together. You might use string, ribbon, twine, raffia, or metal rings.

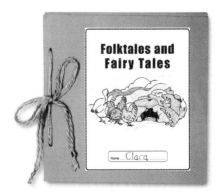

How to Use Literature Pockets
Folktales and Fairy Tales

Step 1

Assemble a blank pocket book for each student. (See page 1.)

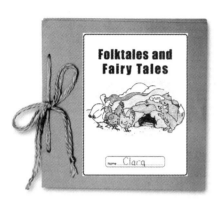

Step 2

Choose the first story you want to study. Reproduce the pocket label/bookmark page for students. Have students color and cut out the label and glue it onto the first pocket in their book.

Step 3

Complete the pocket.

- Have students color and cut out the bookmark and glue it onto a 4½" x 12" (11.5 x 30.5 cm) strip of construction paper. Have them use the bookmark to preview and review the story characters.

- Reproduce the story for students and read it together. Students may track the text with the edge of their bookmark.

- Have students do the follow-up activities and place the paperwork in the pocket with their bookmark and story.

Folktales and Fairy Tales

Name _____

Henny Penny

Pocket Label and Bookmark .... page 5
Have students use these reproducibles to make the Henny Penny pocket label and bookmark. (See page 2.)

The Story of Henny Penny .... pages 6–8
Share and discuss this story of a worried hen who thinks the sky is falling. Reproduce the story on pages 7 and 8 for students. Use the teaching ideas on page 6 to preview, read, and review the story. Follow up with the "More to Explore" activities.

New Friends for Henny Penny .... pages 9–11
Students create an accordion book filled with new rhyming animal names. They tell how these new friends help save Henny Penny and the others.

Henny Penny Finger Puppets .... pages 12 and 13
Students will love using these delightful finger puppets to retell the story of Henny Penny. Have them store the puppets in a resealable plastic bag in the pocket.

A Henny Penny Portrait .... page 14
Students cut, paste, and paint the parts of Henny Penny to create an imaginative picture of the plump hen.

Henny Penny

Story characters:

 Henny Penny

 Cocky Locky

 Ducky Lucky

 Turkey Lurkey

 Foxy Loxy

I liked this story:

☐ Yes

☐ No

This bookmark belongs to

_____
(your name)

Share Henny Penny

Preview the Story

State the title of the story, and have students read aloud the names of the characters listed on the bookmark. Distribute copies of the story (pages 7 and 8), and have students preview the pictures. Invite students who are unfamiliar with the story to predict what happens to Henny Penny and her friends.

Read the Story

Read the story aloud as students follow along. Encourage students to track the text and underline or frame key words. List and discuss any unfamiliar words, such as *ruffled*, *yipped*, *sneaky*, *feasted*, and *squawked*. Point out picture clues and context clues that help explain parts of the story. After you have read the story aloud, encourage students to reread the story independently or with a partner.

Review the Story

Discuss the characters, setting, and plot of the story. Ask questions such as the following to help students recall the sequence of events, identify important details, and draw conclusions:

- Why did Henny Penny think the sky was falling?
- Who was she going to tell about the falling sky?
- Which animal did Henny Penny talk to first? Second? Third? Last?
- Where did the fox take the animals?
- What finally happened to Henny Penny and the other animals?
- What was unusual about the names of the characters in this story?

More to Explore

- Words for *Said*

  Point out to students that the author did not use the word *said* to identify spoken words. Have students skim the story and find the words that were used instead of *said*. (*clucked, crowed, quacked, gobbled, yipped*) Ask students why the author used those words. Then ask them to brainstorm other words that might be used instead of *said* when people are talking in a story.

- Compare and Contrast Different Versions

  Read aloud another version of "Henny Penny." Work with students to compare and contrast the two versions, using a Venn diagram or a comparison chart.

Henny Penny

Henny Penny pecked the ground looking for tasty bugs and worms. A cold wind ruffled her feathers. "On a day like this, anything could happen," she clucked.

Right then, something hard hit her head. "I knew it!" she clucked. "The wind is so wild, it made a piece of the sky fall. I must tell the king!"

Henny Penny ran as fast as a chicken can run. On the other side of the barn, she met Cocky Locky.

"Where are you going in such a hurry?" crowed Cocky Locky. "Slow down!"

"The sky is falling. A piece of it hit my head," clucked Henny Penny. "I'm going to tell the king."

"Really?" crowed Cocky Locky. "I'll help you spread the news."

The two ran on. When they came to the pond, they bumped into Ducky Lucky. "Where are you going in such a hurry?" quacked Ducky Lucky.

"The sky is falling. A piece of it hit my head. We're going to tell the king," clucked Henny Penny.

"I'll waddle along with you," quacked Ducky Lucky. The three of them hurried on.

"Wait!" gobbled a voice by the barn. "Stop, and tell me the news."

"The sky is falling. A piece of it hit my head," clucked Henny Penny. "We're going to tell the king."

"I'll lead the way," gobbled Turkey Lurkey. The four of them ran into the woods.

"Stop!" yipped Foxy Loxy. "Where are you going in such a hurry? Something has happened. I feel it in the air."

"I felt it on my head," clucked Henny Penny. "The sky is falling. We're going to tell the king."

"I know where you can find him," yipped Foxy Loxy. "Follow me!"

Turkey Lurkey, Ducky Lucky, Cocky Locky, and Henny Penny followed Foxy Loxy into a dark cave.

That sneaky fox feasted on turkey, duck, and rooster. He tried to gobble Henny Penny for dessert, but she squawked and flapped her wings. She flew out of the cave and didn't stop running until she was safely back home.

Henny Penny looked up at the sky. It was still there.

Henny Penny

New Friends for Henny Penny

Materials

- pages 10 and 11, reproduced for each student
- 4" x 18" (10 x 45.5 cm) construction paper
- crayons
- scissors
- glue
- stapler

Steps to Follow

❶ Ask students to recall the names of the characters in the story. List the names on the chalkboard and point out the rhyming pattern. Then work with students to list other rhyming animal names. Write the first word of each name on the board, and have volunteers say a rhyme. Students may select from this list of names or think of additional rhyming names as they complete the rest of the activity.

Kitty Mitty	Puppy Luppy
Piggy Wiggy	Hamster Lamster

❷ Have students accordion-fold the construction paper as follows:

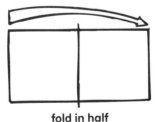

fold in half

fold in half again

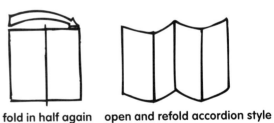

open and refold accordion style

❸ Ask students to choose four animal names to write on their New Friends form. Have them draw a picture of the animal above the name. Then have them cut apart the four sections and glue them onto the folded paper to create a minibook.

❹ Have students cut out the envelope pattern, fold it in half, and staple it along the sides. Students can store their New Friends accordion book in the envelope.

❺ Extend the activity by having students tell a story about how one or more of the new friends helped save Henny Penny and the others.

 Literature Pockets—Folktales and Fairy Tales • EMC 2731

New Friends

A New Friend for
Henny Penny

(friend's name)

A New Friend for
Henny Penny

(friend's name)

A New Friend for
Henny Penny

(friend's name)

A New Friend for
Henny Penny

(friend's name)

New Friends
for
Henny Penny

by _____

fold

Henny Penny Finger Puppets

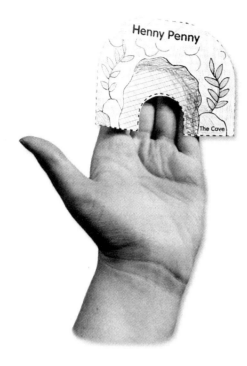

Materials

- page 13, reproduced for each student
- crayons
- scissors
- glue
- resealable plastic bags

Steps to Follow

❶ Guide students through the following steps to make the finger puppets:

a. Color and cut out the puppet pieces.

b. Glue the paper strips as shown to make "rings."

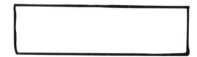

glue

c. Glue the animals to the small rings. Glue the cave to the large ring.

d. Place the cave puppet over one hand and the animal puppets on the fingers of the other hand. Hold the animals next to the cave while retelling the story.

❷ After students use their finger puppets to retell the story, have them put the puppets into a resealable plastic bag and put the bag into the pocket.

Puppet Patterns

Henny Penny

Cocky Locky

Turkey Lurkey

Foxy Loxy

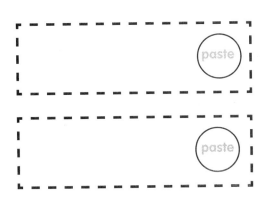

paste

paste

paste

paste

Ducky Lucky

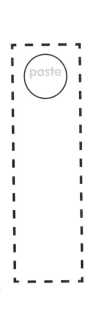

paste

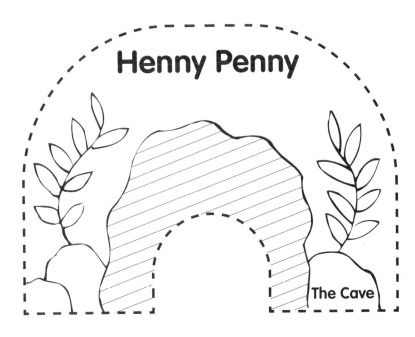

Henny Penny

The Cave

paste

paste

Literature Pockets—Folktales and Fairy Tales • EMC 2731

A Henny Penny Portrait

Materials

- 9" x 12" (23 x 30.5 cm) light blue construction paper
- newspaper
- pie tins
- brown tempera paint, light and dark shades
- scraps of red and yellow construction paper
- scissors
- glue
- crayons or marking pens
- sponge pieces
- writing paper (optional)

Steps to Follow

❶ Cover the work areas with newspaper. Put out pie tins containing brown tempera paint (both light and dark shades).

❷ Guide students through the following steps to make a multi-medium picture of Henny Penny:

a. Draw an outline of the body and head of a hen on the blue construction paper.

b. Spongepaint brown feathers all over the body and head. The side or end of the sponge works well for a feather shape.

c. While the feathers dry, cut out a beak and legs from yellow construction paper and a comb from red construction paper.

d. When the feathers are dry, glue the beak, legs, and comb in place. Add an eye with a crayon or marking pen.

e. If you want, add background details to show a scene from the story.

❸ Extend the activity by having students write a description of Henny Penny. Students may glue the written description onto the back of the picture.

The Brave Little Tailor

Pocket Label and Bookmark .... page 16

Have students use these reproducibles to make The Brave Little Tailor pocket label and bookmark. (See page 2.)

The Story of
The Brave Little Tailor .... pages 17–19

Share and discuss this story of a brave little tailor who outwits three strong giants. Reproduce the story on pages 18 and 19 for students. Use the teaching ideas on page 17 to preview, read, and review the story. Follow up with the "More to Explore" activities.

The Brave Little Tailor
Mobile .... pages 20–22

Students create a colorful mobile of shapes and sentences to tell how the little tailor tricked the giants.

Sequence a Story Belt... pages 23 and 24

Sequencing a story becomes a whole new experience when students "stitch" together a belt that shows what happened to the little tailor.

The Job of a Tailor .... page 25

Have students color, cut out, and fold these minipages to make a little nonfiction book that tells how a tailor makes clothes.

The Brave Little Tailor

Story characters:

 Little Tailor

 First Giant

 Second Giant

 Third Giant

 King

 Princess

I liked this story:

☐ Yes

☐ No

This bookmark belongs to

_____

(your name)

Share The Brave Little Tailor

Preview the Story

State the title of the story, and have students read aloud the names of the characters listed on the bookmark. Distribute copies of the story (pages 18 and 19), and have students preview the pictures. Invite students who are unfamiliar with the story to predict what the phrase "seven at one blow" means in the story.

Read the Story

Read the story aloud as students follow along. Encourage students to track the text and underline or frame key words. List and discuss any unfamiliar words, such as *swarmed*, *stitched*, *palace*, *acorn*, and *highness*. Point out picture clues and context clues that help explain parts of the story. After you have read the story aloud, encourage students to reread the story independently or with a partner.

Review the Story

Discuss the characters, setting, and plot of the story. Ask questions such as the following to help students recall important details, draw conclusions, summarize, and identify character traits:

- How did the flies get into the tailor's workroom?
- What words did the tailor stitch on his belt? What did the words mean?
- When the giants and the king read the words on the belt, what did they think it meant?
- What did the king want the tailor to do? What did he promise the tailor?
- How did the tailor fool the giants?
- How would you describe the tailor?

More to Explore

- Brave Deeds

  Point out to students that the tailor used his brain to beat the giants. Ask students to think about a brave deed they have done that required them to use their brain. Invite students to share their experiences or write about them in their journals.

- Exaggerations

  Remind students that the first giant was so strong he could squeeze water out of a stone. He could also throw a stone so high that it touched a cloud. Have students tell their own exaggerated statements of strength, speed, and endurance. Have them complete the following sentence frame by adding a name, a verb, and a description: *My _____ _____ so strong/high/fast/far that _____.*

- Compare and Contrast Different Versions

  Read aloud another version of "The Brave Little Tailor." Work with students to compare and contrast the two versions, using a Venn diagram or a comparison chart.

The Brave Little Tailor

A busy little tailor set his jelly sandwich near an open window. "I will sew this pair of pants before I eat," he said.

While he stitched, flies swarmed over the sandwich. The tailor hit the flies with his cutting board. "Seven dead flies," he said. "I will tell everyone."

The tailor stitched the words *Seven With One Blow* on his belt. Then he put some cheese in his pocket and went for a walk.

Along the way, the tailor found a bird in a bush. He put the bird in his pocket with the cheese.

In the forest, the tailor saw a giant cutting a tree. "Giant, see my belt? I killed seven with one blow."

Literature Pockets—Folktales and Fairy Tales • EMC 2731

The giant laughed at the little tailor. "I'm much stronger than you," he said. He squeezed a stone so hard that water ran out of it.

"Not bad," said the tailor. "But I can squeeze milk from my stone." The tailor squeezed milk from his cheese.

The giant was surprised but wasn't ready to give up. He threw a stone into the sky. The stone went so high it touched a cloud and came down.

"Watch this," said the tailor. He took the bird from his pocket and the bird flew away. "My stone flew so high that it didn't come down."

"You win," said the giant.

The tailor smiled as he went on his way. Soon he came to a palace. "See my belt?" said the tailor to the king.

The king read *Seven With One Blow.* "You are stronger than my army," said the king. "There are two giants in the forest. They steal our food and destroy our homes. If you kill them, you shall have half my kingdom and marry my daughter."

The tailor found the two giants sleeping under an oak tree. The tailor climbed the tree. He dropped an acorn on the face of one snoring giant. The giant woke up. "Stop that!" he said.

"I did nothing," said the other giant.

Soon the giants were snoring again. The tailor threw more acorns, waking both giants. The angry giants began to fight. They hit each other so hard that they both fell dead.

The tailor went back to the king. "Your highness, the giants are dead. The soldiers will find them in the forest."

The king put a crown on the little tailor's head. "Half of my kingdom is yours. Tomorrow you will marry my daughter." And he did.

The Brave Little Tailor Mobile

Materials

- pages 21 and 22, reproduced for each student
- three 6" square (13 cm) pieces of construction paper
- 5" x 2½" (13 x 6.5 cm) construction paper
- four 6" (15 cm) pieces of string
- crayons
- scissors
- glue
- hole punch

Steps to Follow

❶ Ask students to recall how the brave little tailor fooled the giants. Have them write on each reproduced shape a brief description of how the item was used.

❷ Have students color and cut out the four shapes and glue them onto construction paper. Have them cut out the shapes again, leaving a border.

❸ Help students punch holes in the shapes as marked. Have them tie the shapes together with string to make a mobile. Be sure they put the title piece first.

❹ Encourage more advanced students to make additional shapes for their mobiles. Students may draw and write about other items the tailor could have used to fool the giants.

❺ Display the mobiles for everyone to see. After the display comes down, store the mobiles in students' pockets.

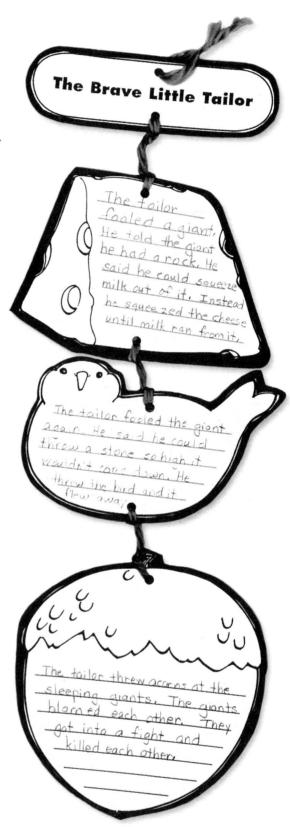

The Brave Little Tailor

Mobile Shapes

Sequence a Story Belt

Materials
- page 24, reproduced for each student
- sentence strips
- crayons
- scissors
- glue
- hole punch
- yarn

Steps to Follow

❶ Have students color and cut apart the sequence cards.

❷ Ask students to glue the cards close together in correct sequence onto a sentence strip. Have them trim off the excess part of the strip.

❸ Have students punch holes along the top and bottom of the sentence strip. (You may choose to punch the holes for students in advance or while they work.)

❹ Give each student two long strands of yarn. Each strand should be about a foot longer than the sentence strip. Have students weave one strand through the holes on one end of the strip and weave the other strand through the holes at the other end of the strip. Tie the yarn at each end to hold it in place.

❺ Have students help each other tie the belts around their waists. After students have had an opportunity to show off their belts, have them put the belts (folded) into their pocket.

**The Brave
Little Tailor**

Sequence Cards

A tailor makes clothes for people.

The Job of a Tailor

①

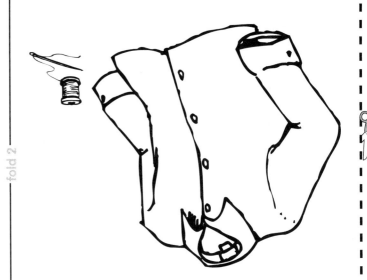

A tailor sews the pieces together. Then the tailor sews on buttons, zippers, and trim.

④

A tailor uses different tools and equipment to make the clothes.

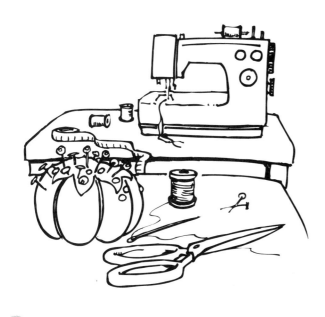

②

A tailor pins a pattern to cloth and cuts out the pieces.

③

The Fisherman and His Wife

Pocket Label and Bookmark........page 27
Have students use these reproducibles to make The Fisherman and His Wife pocket label and bookmark. (See page 2.)

The Story of The Fisherman and His Wife..........................pages 28–30
Share and discuss this story of a magic fish who tries to fulfill the greedy demands of a fisherman's wife. Reproduce the story on pages 29 and 30 for students. Use the teaching ideas on page 28 to preview, read, and review the story. Follow up with the "More to Explore" activities.

What Did They Say? ....pages 31 and 32
For this sequencing activity, students cut and paste dialog into speech bubbles and organize pictures in a minibook to show the correct sequence of events.

A Magic Fish.................................page 33
With a little stuffing, a golden crown, and some colorful details, students create a stuffed fish that looks "magical."

What Would You Wish For?..........page 34
Students write and illustrate what they would wish for if they caught a magic fish. Remind students to give reasons for their choices. Encourage them to consider the lesson they learned from the story as they decide on their own wishes.

The Fisherman and His Wife

Story characters:

 Fisherman

 Fisherman's Wife

 Magic Fish

I liked this story:

☐ Yes

☐ No

This bookmark belongs to

_____

(your name)

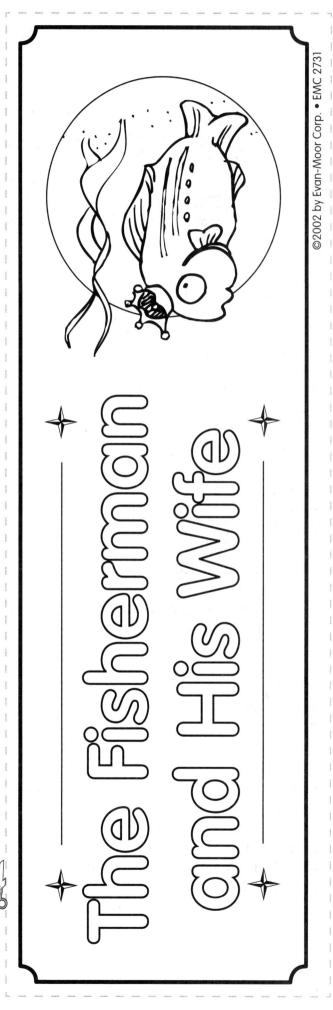

The Fisherman and His Wife

Share The Fisherman and His Wife

Preview the Story

State the title of the story, and have students read aloud the names of the characters listed on the bookmark. Distribute copies of the story (pages 29 and 30), and have students preview the pictures. Invite students who are unfamiliar with the story to predict what happens when the fisherman catches a magic fish.

Read the Story

Read the story aloud as students follow along. Encourage students to track the text and underline or frame key words. List and discuss any unfamiliar words, such as *crown*, *enchanted*, *cottage*, *servants*, and *rule*. Point out picture clues and context clues that help explain parts of the story. After you have read the story aloud, encourage students to reread the story independently or with a partner.

Review the Story

Discuss the characters, setting, and plot of the story. Ask questions such as the following to help students recall important details, draw conclusions, and share opinions:

- What was special about the fish that the fisherman caught?
- What did the magic fish ask the fisherman to do?
- What were the fisherman's wife's three wishes?
- What did the magic fish do when the fisherman's wife asked to rule the sun and the moon?
- Why do you think the magic fish took everything away?
- How do you think the fisherman's wife felt when she was back in the hut?

More to Explore

- An Enchanted Prince

  The magic fish said he was an enchanted prince. Invite students to share their opinions about how and why the prince was changed into a fish. Then have them suggest ways the magic spell might be broken.

- To, Too, Two

  Point out to students that the words *to, too,* and *two* sound the same but are spelled differently and have different meanings. Give examples of how to use each word. Ask students which word was used by the fisherman when he responded to his wife. Then invite students to say their own sentences that include the word *to, too,* or *two*. Have them say sentences about the story.

- Compare and Contrast Different Versions

  Read aloud another version of "The Fisherman and His Wife." Work with students to compare and contrast the two versions, using a Venn diagram or a comparison chart.

The Fisherman and His Wife

The Fisherman and His Wife

Long ago there was a fisherman who caught a magic fish.

"See my crown?" said the fish. "I'm an enchanted prince. Please let me go."

That's just what the fisherman did. Then he ran home to tell his wife. "I caught a magic fish!" he told her.

"What did the fish give you?" asked the wife.

"Nothing," said the fisherman.

"Ask him for a new cottage," said the wife. "After all, you saved his life."

"That's too much!" said the fisherman.

The fisherman's wife would not be quiet. So the fisherman went back to the lake. "Magic fish," he called. "My wife wishes for a cottage."

The magic fish jumped from the water. "It's done," he said.

The fisherman thanked the fish and ran home to his new cottage.

The fisherman's wife was happy for a year and a day. Then she said, "Ask the fish for a grand palace with servants and a table covered with food."

"That's too much!" said the fisherman.

The fisherman's wife would not be quiet. So the fisherman went back to the lake. "Magic fish," he called. "My wife wants to be queen with a palace and servants and a table covered with food."

"It's done," said the fish.

The fisherman thanked the fish and went home to the palace.

The fisherman's wife was happy for a year and a day. Then she said, "Husband, the sun and the moon are higher than I am. Tell the fish I want to rule everything."

"That's too much!" said the fisherman.

The fisherman's wife would not be quiet. So the fisherman went back to the lake. "My wife wants to rule the sun and the moon," he told the magic fish.

The fisherman waited and waited, but the fish didn't answer. When the fisherman reached home, he found his wife sweeping their old hut.

What Did They Say?

Materials

- page 32, reproduced for each student
- 4" x 18" (10 x 45.5 cm) construction paper
- crayons
- scissors
- glue
- hole punch
- 24" (61 cm) pieces of string or yarn

Steps to Follow

❶ Guide students through the following steps to make a minibook:

a. Accordion-fold the construction paper.

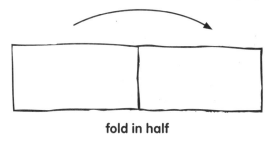

fold in half

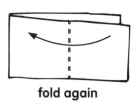

fold again

open and fold
accordion style

b. Color and cut out the pictures. Glue the first box on the cover of the accordion book. Glue the remaining boxes on the other pages.

c. Cut out the speech bubbles and glue them to the correct pictures to show what the fisherman's wife said each time.

❷ Invite students to read their books to a partner.

Variation

Have more advanced students create their own original minibook. Have students follow the same basic steps, but have them use a 4" x 36" (10 x 91.5 cm) strip of construction paper and fold it in half one more time to make an eight-page book. Students may use the folded strip as a template to cut out blank pages.

The Fisherman and His Wife

A Magic Fish

Materials

- 9" x 12" (23 x 30.5 cm) white construction paper
- 4" square (10 cm) gold construction paper or gold foil
- crayons and marking pens
- scraps of colored construction paper
- shredded paper or thin strips of newspaper (for stuffing)
- copy paper
- scissors
- paper clips
- glue
- several staplers

Steps to Follow

❶ Draw a large outline of a fish and a smaller outline of a crown (about 3" or 8 cm wide) on one sheet of copy paper. Reproduce the templates for students.

❷ Guide students through the following steps to make a stuffed fish:

   a. Cut out the fish template. Place it on top of two sheets of construction paper and trace it. You can use a paper clip to hold the template in place.

   b. Cut out the fish.

   c. Lay the two pieces face to face, as if they are looking at each other. Use crayons, marking pens, and paper scraps to decorate them exactly the same.

   d. Staple the tail section of the fish together along the edge. (The decorated sides should be showing.) Stuff the tail with paper strips.

   e. Staple along the top and bottom of the fish and stuff the body with paper strips.

   f. Staple around the mouth area to close off the fish.

   g. Cut out the crown template. Trace it onto gold paper. Cut out the gold crown and glue it onto the fish's head.

❸ Invite students to use their "magic fish" to retell the story or tell about another adventure for the fish.

Variation

Provide glitter, sequins, wiggle eyes, and other decorative items for students to use.

The Fisherman and His Wife

Note: Reproduce this page for each student. Use the directions given on page 26 to help students complete the activity.

Name: ______________________________

What Would You Wish For?

If I caught a magic fish, I would wish for ______________________

because ______________________________________

____

____

____

____

____

Here is a picture of my wish.

Jack and the Beanstalk

Pocket Label and Bookmark .... page 36
Have students use these reproducibles to make the Jack and the Beanstalk pocket label and bookmark. (See page 2.)

The Story of Jack and the Beanstalk .... pages 37–39
Share and discuss this story of a needy boy who discovers some treasures and a giant at the top of a magic beanstalk. Reproduce the story on pages 38 and 39 for students. Use the teaching ideas on page 37 to preview, read, and review the story. Follow up with the "More to Explore" activities.

Folded Beanstalk ....pages 40 and 41
Students' math skills "grow" as they make and measure a giant beanstalk.

Watch Jack Climb the Beanstalk .... pages 42–44
Students will love creating and using this movable storyboard. Have them move Jack up and down the beanstalk to show him carrying off the giant's treasures.

What Would the Harp Say? .... page 45
Students consider the harp's point of view as they complete this writing activity. Provide the following writing prompts: What did the harp observe about Jack and the giant? What does she think about their actions? How does she feel about being "kidnapped"? Encourage more advanced students to express the harp's thoughts and feelings in the form of a song.

Jack and the Beanstalk

Story characters:

 Jack

 Jack's Mother

 Old Man

 Giant

 Magic Hen

 Magic Harp

I liked this story:

☐ Yes

☐ No

This bookmark belongs to

_____

(your name)

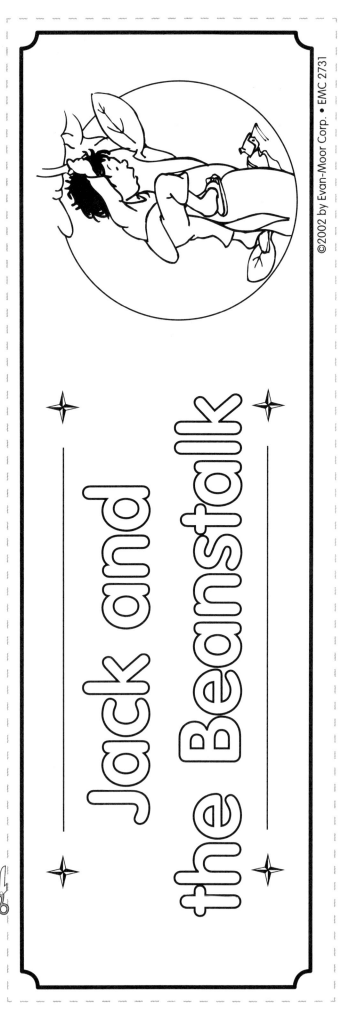

Share Jack and the Beanstalk

Preview the Story

State the title of the story, and have students read aloud the names of the characters listed on the bookmark. Distribute copies of the story (pages 38 and 39), and have students preview the pictures. Invite students who are unfamiliar with the story to predict what Jack discovers at the top of a giant beanstalk.

Read the Story

Read the story aloud as students follow along. Encourage students to track the text and underline or frame key words. List and discuss any unfamiliar words, such as *foolish*, *harp*, *headed*, *scrambled*, and *toppled*. Point out picture clues and context clues that help explain parts of the story. After you have read the story aloud, encourage students to reread the story independently or with a partner.

Review the Story

Discuss the characters, setting, and plot of the story. Ask questions such as the following to help students recall the sequence of events, draw conclusions, and make judgments:

- Why did Jack and his mother have to sell their cow?
- Why do you think Jack's mother was so angry when she saw the beans?
- What happened to the beans overnight?
- What did Jack find when he climbed the beanstalk?
- Name the things Jack brought back on each of his trips up the beanstalk.
- Why was the giant so angry at Jack?
- Do you think it right or wrong of Jack to take the giant's belongings? Explain your answer.

More to Explore

- Words with /ō/ or /ou/

  Have students listen for words that have the /ō/ sound as you reread the story aloud. Have them keep a tally of the words they hear. After reading, list the words on the chalkboard. *(no, told, so, old, home, show, opened, gold, woke, below, followed)* Point out the different spellings for the sound. Have students find each word in the story and compare the total to their tallies. Then repeat the process for words that have /ou/ as in *house. (house, cow, town, out, outside, down, found, ground)*

- Grow a Beanstalk

  Connect literature and science by having students plant their own beans. Use clear plastic disposable cups (soft plastic) for the containers so students can observe different stages of the sprouting seed. Have students monitor the plant's growth and write or draw their observations in a small journal. Students may store their completed journal in their pocket.

- Compare and Contrast Different Versions

  Read aloud another version of "Jack and the Beanstalk." Work with students to compare and contrast the two versions, using a Venn diagram or a comparison chart.

Jack and the Beanstalk

Jack and the Beanstalk

Jack and his mother were hungry and there was no food in the house. Jack's mother told Jack to take the cow to town and sell it. "Be quick, Jack," said his mother.

So Jack led the cow away. On his way to town he met an old man. "Sell me your cow," said the man. "I will give you these magic beans for her."

Jack remembered his mother's words, "Be quick!" He gave the old man the cow and took the magic beans. He hurried home to show them to his mother.

Jack's mother looked up from her cleaning as Jack opened the door. "How much did you get for the cow?" she asked. Jack held out his hand and showed her the beans.

"Only a handful of beans? You foolish boy. How will we buy food? What will we eat?" she cried.

Jack looked at the beans in his hand. "But Mother, these are magic beans."

"Magic beans? Jack, there is no such thing as magic beans." She threw the beans out the window. Once again, Jack and his mother went to bed with empty stomachs.

The next morning, Jack's growling stomach woke him early. He looked outside and saw a giant beanstalk in the garden. He ran to the beanstalk and climbed it. At the top he found a huge castle.

Jack crawled up the steps and squeezed under the door of the castle. He saw a sleeping giant. Near the giant was a bag of gold. Jack moved quietly to the giant's side and grabbed the gold. He ran back to the beanstalk and climbed down.

The gold lasted for many days. When it was gone, Jack climbed back up the beanstalk. This time he found a hen that laid gold eggs. Jack carried the hen back to his mother.

After many months, Jack decided to climb the beanstalk one more time. A magic harp was singing for the giant. The music had put the giant to sleep. Jack grabbed the harp and headed for the beanstalk. The harp started to yell for help. This woke the giant.

The angry giant ran after Jack. Jack scrambled down the beanstalk. The giant followed him. The beanstalk shook with each giant step. Jack called to his mother below to get the ax. He slid to the ground and began chopping the beanstalk. Just as the giant's foot came into view, the beanstalk toppled. The giant smashed to the ground. Jack's magic beanstalk was gone.

Folded Beanstalk

Materials

- page 41, reproduced for each student
- 32" (81 cm) strip of cash register tape for each student
- green and red crayons
- rulers
- paper clips

Steps to Follow

❶ Guide students through the following steps to make a beanstalk:

a. Draw a thick green line down the length of the paper strip. This line is the stalk of the beanstalk. Draw large and small leaves along the stalk.

b. Accordion-fold the stalk by folding the strip in half three times and then refolding it back and forth as shown.

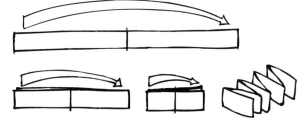

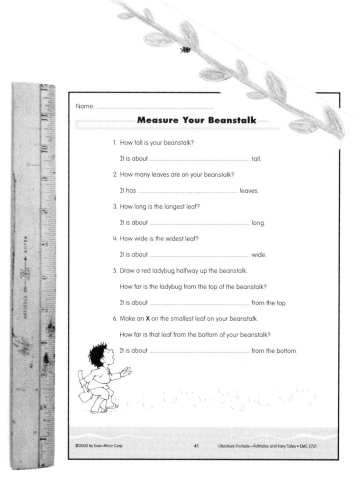

c. Open the beanstalk and use it to complete the Measure Your Beanstalk worksheet.

❷ Monitor students as they use rulers, their beanstalks, and red crayons to complete the worksheet. Have more advanced students determine the lengths in both standard and metric units, measuring to the nearest inch or centimeter. Encourage students to estimate the values before they measure them.

❸ Have students paper-clip their folded beanstalks to their completed worksheets.

❹ Extend the activity by having partners exchange papers and check each other's measurements.

Name: _____

Measure Your Beanstalk

1. How tall is your beanstalk?

   It is about _____ tall.

2. How many leaves are on your beanstalk?

   It has _____ leaves.

3. How long is the longest leaf?

   It is about _____ long.

4. How wide is the widest leaf?

   It is about _____ wide.

5. Draw a red ladybug halfway up the beanstalk.

   How far is the ladybug from the top of the beanstalk?

   It is about _____ from the top.

6. Make an **X** on the smallest leaf on your beanstalk.

   How far is that leaf from the bottom of your beanstalk?

   It is about _____ from the bottom.

Watch Jack Climb the Beanstalk

Materials

- pages 43 and 44, reproduced for each student
- 12" x 18" (30.5 x 45.5 cm) construction paper
- 2" x 4" (5 x 10 cm) construction paper
- crayons
- glue
- scissors
- hole punch
- small envelopes
- 24" (61 cm) piece of string
- tape
- small self-stick notes

Steps to Follow

❶ Guide students through the following steps:

a. Fold the large construction paper into thirds.

b. Color the beanstalk and glue the sheet onto the center section of the construction paper.

c. Punch out the two holes.

d. Color and cut out Jack. Glue him onto the small construction paper and trim it. Punch the holes as indicated.

e. Thread the string through the holes in Jack. Put the same string through the holes in the beanstalk. Then tie the string in the back of the beanstalk. To move Jack up and down the beanstalk, pull the string.

f. Color and cut out the house and castle. Glue the house to the lower left-hand side of the construction paper. Glue the castle onto the upper right-hand side.

g. Glue an envelope under the castle on the right-hand side. This will be used to store all pieces when they are not in use.

h. Color and cut out the rest of the characters. Fold the giant to stand him up. Tape the other characters onto self-stick notes.

❷ Use the beanstalk to retell the story. Show Jack moving up the beanstalk to get each item. Stick the item onto Jack. Then show Jack moving down the beanstalk to take the item home. Jack will need to go up and down the beanstalk several times to complete the story.

Character Patterns

43

Character Patterns

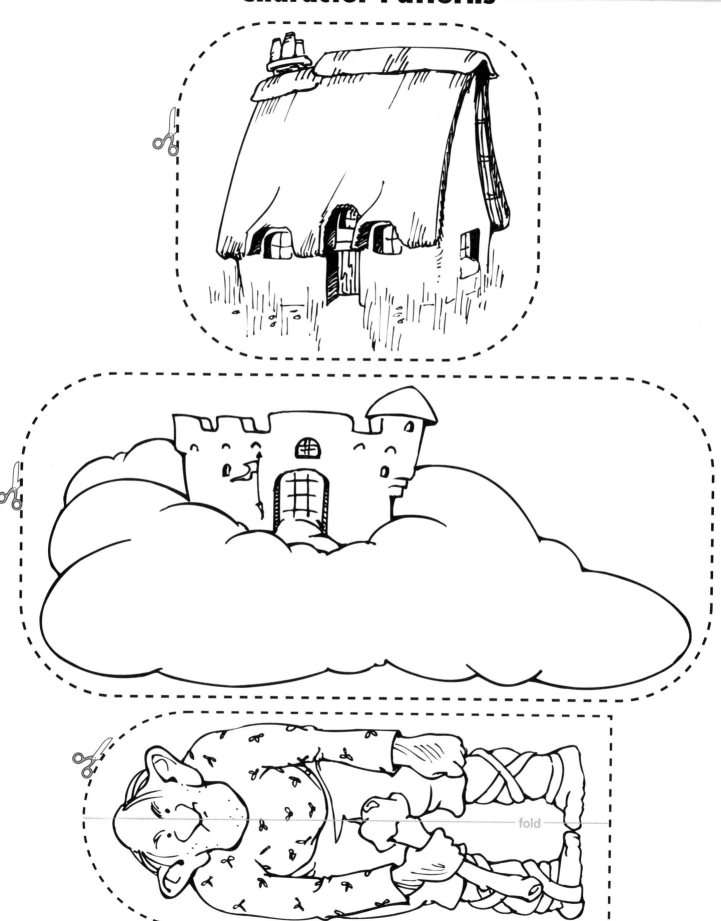

fold

Literature Pockets—Folktales and Fairy Tales • EMC 2731

Note: Reproduce this page for each student. Use the directions given on page 35 to help students complete the activity.

Name: _____

What Would the Harp Say?

What do you think the harp would say about Jack and the giant? Write about it.

The Elves and the Shoemaker

Pocket Label and Bookmark ....**page 47**
Have students use these reproducibles to make The Elves and the Shoemaker pocket label and bookmark. (See page 2.)

The Story of The Elves and the Shoemaker ....**pages 48–50**
Share and discuss this story of two little elves who help a kindhearted shoemaker. Reproduce the story on pages 49 and 50 for students. Use the teaching ideas on page 48 to preview, read, and review the story. Follow up with the "More to Explore" activities.

A Kind Heart................... **pages 51 and 52**
Both the shoemaker and the elves had kind hearts and helped others. Students make heart shapes and write about someone they know with a kind heart.

What Did They See? .... **pages 53–55**
Students lift the flaps of this minibook to see who is hiding behind the curtain and who is making the shoes each night.

Dress an Elf..................... **pages 56 and 57**
Using scraps of paper or cloth, students create an outfit for a little elf.

A Shoe Encyclopedia .... **pages 58–60**
So many shoes! Students put together a little shoe encyclopedia.

The Elves and the Shoemaker

Story characters:

 Shoemaker

 Shoemaker's Wife

 Rich Gentleman

 Elves

I liked this story:

☐ Yes

☐ No

This bookmark belongs to

_____

(your name)

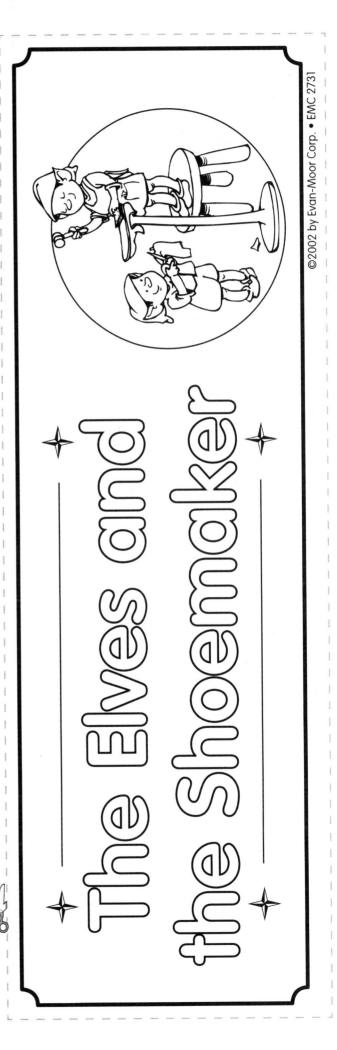

The Elves and the Shoemaker

Share The Elves and the Shoemaker

Preview the Story

State the title of the story, and have students read aloud the names of the characters listed on the bookmark. Distribute copies of the story (pages 49 and 50), and have students preview the pictures. Invite students who are unfamiliar with the story to predict how the elves and the shoemaker get along in the story.

Read the Story

Read the story aloud as students follow along. Encourage students to track the text and underline or frame key words. List and discuss any unfamiliar words, such as *village*, *poor*, *leather*, *workbench*, and *curtain*. Point out picture clues and context clues that help explain parts of the story. After you have read the story aloud, encourage students to reread the story independently or with a partner.

Review the Story

Discuss the characters, setting, and plot of the story. Ask questions such as the following to help students recall important details, draw conclusions, summarize, and identify character traits:

- What was the shoemaker's problem?
- What surprise did the shoemaker find in the morning?
- How did the shoemaker and his wife find out who was making the shoes?
- How did the shoemaker and his wife thank the elves?
- The story says "the shoemaker and his wife were no longer poor." How did this happen?
- How did the shoemaker show that he was kind? How did the elves show that they were kind?

More to Explore

- Thank You

  The shoemaker and his wife made clothing and shoes for the elves. Ask students to think of other ways they might have thanked the elves.

- Time Order

  Point out to students that the story includes time-order words and phrases that help them keep track of when the events happened. Have students identify those words and phrases in the story. *(one evening, the next morning, soon, that day, every night, at midnight, the next day, that night)*

- Compare and Contrast Different Versions

  Read aloud another version of "The Elves and the Shoemaker." Work with students to compare and contrast the two versions, using a Venn diagram or a comparison chart.

The Elves and the Shoemaker

A kind shoemaker made shoes for the children in his village. Some children needed shoes but had no money. He gave them shoes anyway. Because of his kind heart, he became poorer and poorer.

One evening the shoemaker said to his wife, "I only have enough leather to make one more pair of shoes. We have no money to buy more leather."

"What will be, will be," said his wife. "Make the last pair of shoes in the morning. Someone will buy the shoes."

The next morning when they returned to work, the shoemaker and his wife found a pair of shoes on the workbench. "Who made these shoes?" asked the wife.

"Not I," said the shoemaker.

Soon a rich gentleman came into the shop. "What a fine pair of shoes," he said and gave the shoemaker four gold coins for them.

The Elves and
the Shoemaker

"Now I can buy leather for four pairs of shoes," the shoemaker told his wife. He went to the market and bought the leather. He left leather for four pairs of shoes on the workbench.

The next morning the shoemaker found four pairs of shoes on the workbench. Before long, those shoes were sold. Every night the shoemaker left out leather for shoes. Every morning he found more shoes. Soon his moneybox was full of coins.

"Who is helping us? How can we thank them?" asked the wife.

"Tonight we shall see for ourselves," said the shoemaker. The shoemaker cut the pieces of leather and left them on the workbench. Then he and his wife hid behind the curtain.

At midnight two elves skipped into the room. They sang as they sewed. When the shoes were finished, they danced around the room and out the door.

"Poor little ones," said the wife. "They have no clothes."

"Their bare feet must be cold," said the shoemaker.

The next day the shoemaker and his wife cut and sewed. That night they set out warm clothes and two pairs of little shoes. Once again they hid behind the curtain.

When the elves saw the clothes and shoes, they put them on while singing, "What a surprise! What a treat! Soft, warm clothes. Shoes for our feet!" Then they skipped out the door and never came back.

Because the elves had helped them, the shoemaker and his wife were no longer poor. They still made shoes, working happily ever after. And sometimes they wondered about those helpful elves.

A Kind Heart

outside

inside

Materials
- page 52, reproduced for each student
- writing paper
- crayons
- scissors
- stapler

Steps to Follow

❶ Have students color and cut out the heart pattern and fold it in half as indicated. Then have them use the folded heart as a template, tracing it onto a sheet of writing paper and cutting out the lined heart.

❷ Ask students to write about someone they know with a kind heart, describing something kind the person has done.

❸ Have students staple the written page inside the heart cover.

❹ Invite students to read their descriptions aloud.

The Elves and
the Shoemaker

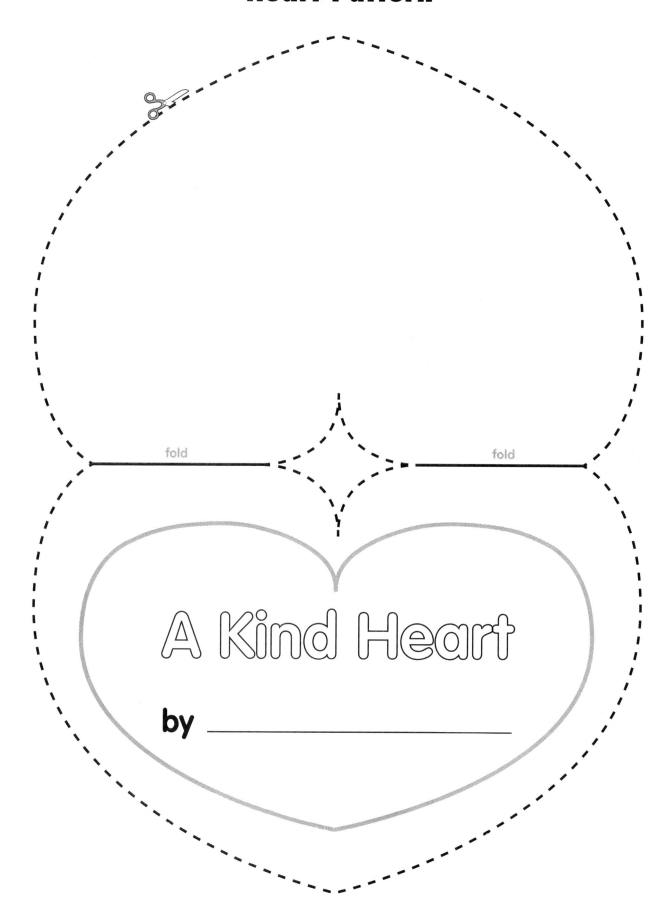

fold

fold

A Kind Heart

by _____

What Did They See?

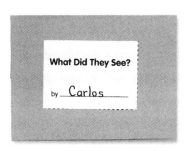

Materials

- pages 54 and 55, reproduced for each student
- 9" x 12" (23 x 30.5 cm) construction paper
- 4" x 7" (10 x 18 cm) colorful lightweight fabric
- scissors
- crayons or marking pens
- glue
- two-sided tape (optional)

Steps to Follow

❶ Work with students to complete the following steps to make a flap book. Demonstrate each step:

a. Fold the construction paper into fourths. Then open it and cut out the top left-hand section.

b. Color and cut out the pictures.

c. Glue the pictures onto the construction paper. Glue the shoemaker and his wife to the top right-hand section. Glue the elves to the bottom right-hand section. Then fold over the bottom left-hand section and glue on the workbench.

d. Place a strip of two-sided tape (or use glue) across the top of the section with the shoemaker and his wife. Press the piece of fabric to this section to make a curtain. (If you use glue, allow it to dry.)

e. Write an answer to the question "What did they see?" on the lined form. Then cut out the answer box and the question box.

f. Fold down the top section of the flap book. Glue the question box to the construction paper. Turn the book over and glue the answer box to the back.

❷ Invite students to show their flap books to classmates.

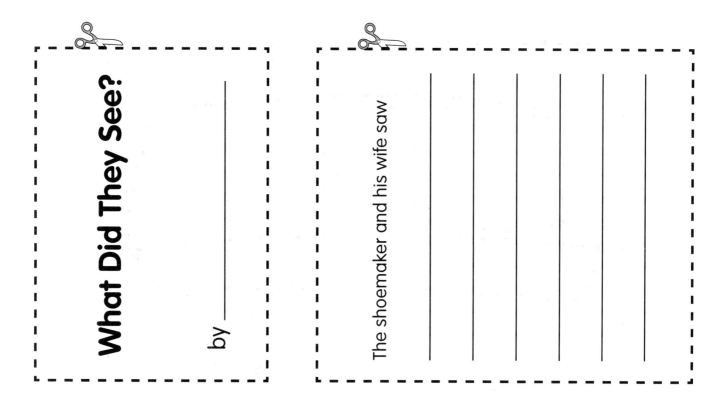

What Did They See?

by _____

The shoemaker and his wife saw

What Did They See?

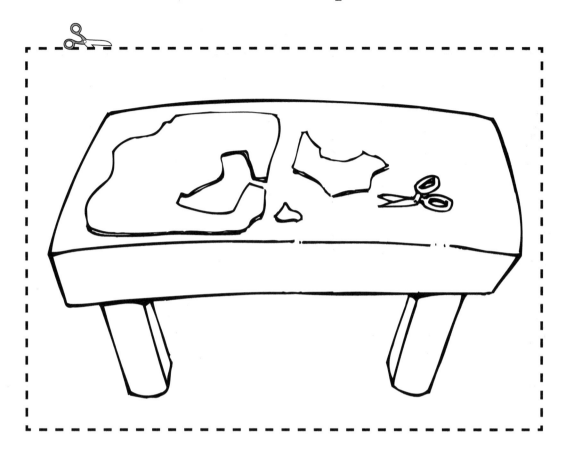

Dress an Elf

Materials

- page 57, reproduced for each student
- assorted scraps of fabric or construction paper
- scissors
- glue
- crayons or marking pens

Steps to Follow

❶ Discuss what an elf might wear. Then demonstrate how to lay the elf pattern on a piece of fabric or paper and trace a piece of clothing such as trousers or a shirt.

❷ Invite students to use fabric or paper scraps to dress their elves. Remind them to include shoes. Have them use crayons or marking pens to add facial features and other small details.

❸ Have an elf fashion show! Display the elves and have students compare and contrast them. Afterward, have students put their elves into the pocket.

❹ Extend the activity by having students write on the back of their elves how they made the outfit.

The Elves and the Shoemaker

Elf Pattern

57

A Shoe Encyclopedia

Materials
- pages 59 and 60, reproduced for each student
- 4" x 9" (10 x 20 cm) construction paper
- shoelaces or string
- scissors
- crayons
- hole punch

Steps to Follow

❶ Lead students in a discussion about shoes. Work together to brainstorm different kinds of shoes, such as seasonal shoes (rain boots, snow boots, sandals), everyday shoes (sneakers, cowboy boots, high-heel pumps, bedroom slippers, dress shoes), and sports shoes (baseball cleats, tennis shoes, bowling shoes, ice skates, ballet slippers, tap shoes, hiking boots). List the shoes on the chalkboard.

❷ Read aloud the names of the shoes shown on the shoe cards. Discuss who might wear each kind of shoe.

❸ Have students color the shoe cards and write a sentence for each one telling who would wear the shoe and when it would be worn. For the last card, have students decide on their own shoe, draw a picture of it, and complete the sentence. Refer students to the list of shoes on the board.

❹ Ask students to cut apart the shoe cards and put them in a stack. Ask more advanced students to put their cards in alphabetical order.

❺ Have students fold the construction paper in half to form the cover. Have them glue the title card onto the cover.

❻ After students put the shoe cards inside the cover, have them punch two holes in the left side of the book and tie the pages together with a shoelace or string.

❼ Extend the activity by having students use magazine cutouts of shoes to make additional pages for their books. Students may use their book as a template, tracing the book onto white paper and cutting out the boxes to make additional blank pages.

The Elves and the Shoemaker

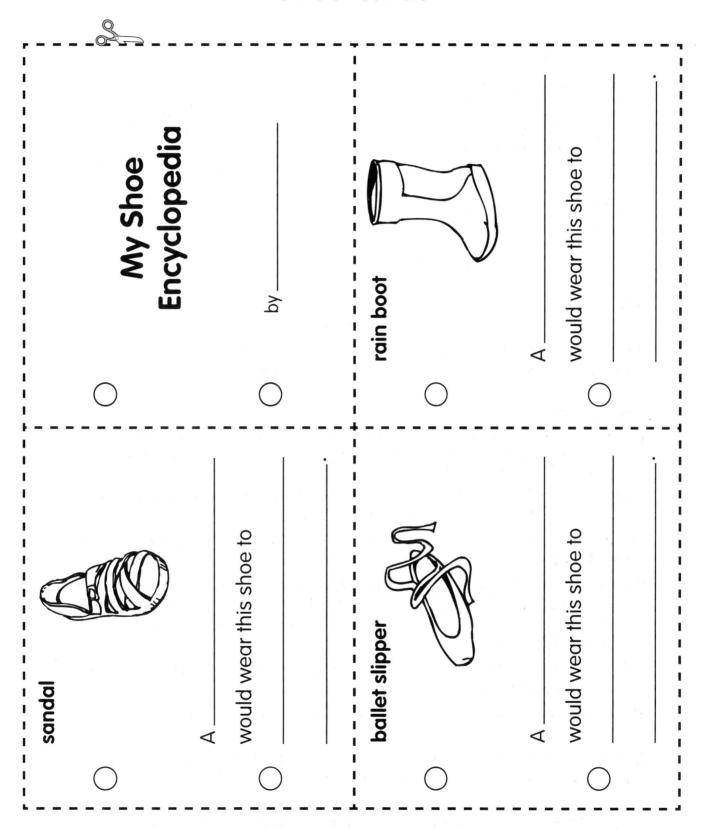

My Shoe Encyclopedia

by _____

rain boot

A _____ would wear this shoe to _____.

sandal

A _____ would wear this shoe to _____.

ballet slipper

A _____ would wear this shoe to _____.

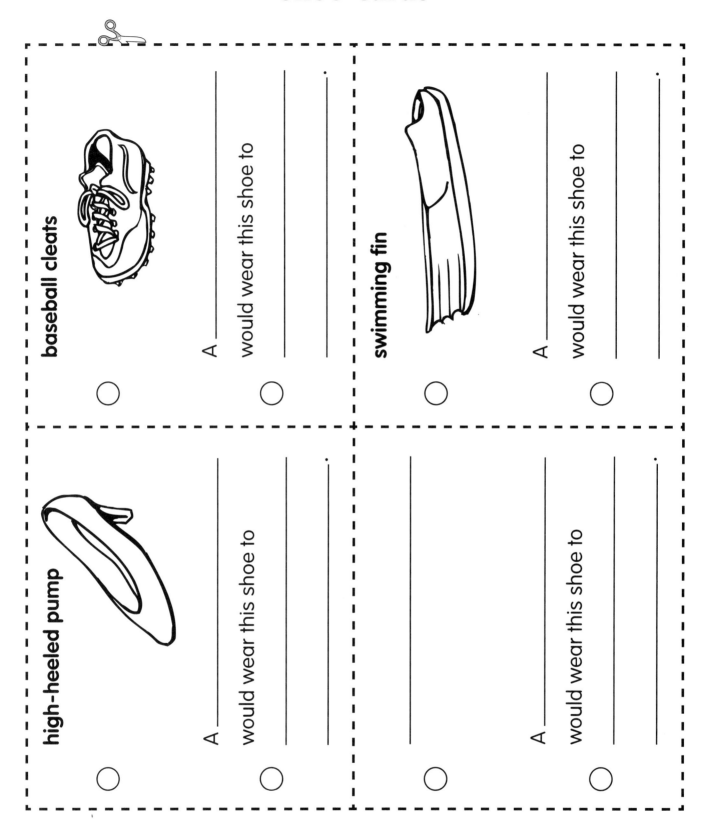

baseball cleats

○

A _____

would wear this shoe to _____

○ _____

.

swimming fin

○

A _____

would wear this shoe to _____

○ _____

.

high-heeled pump

○

A _____

would wear this shoe to _____

○ _____

.

○

A _____

would wear this shoe to _____

○ _____

.

The Frog Prince

Pocket Label and Bookmark ....page 62
Have students use these reproducibles to make The Frog Prince pocket label and bookmark. (See page 2.)

**The Story of
The Frog Prince.....................pages 63–65**
Share and discuss this story of an enchanted frog who persuades a pampered princess to take care of him. Reproduce the story on pages 64 and 65 for students. Use the teaching ideas on page 63 to preview, read, and review the story. Follow up with the "More to Explore" activities.

A Crafty Frog Prince ....pages 66–68
Students change a few sheets of construction paper into an adorable frog prince holding the princess's golden ball. On the back of the frog, have students write what the frog might say about the princess.

**A Promise Is a
Promise...........................pages 69 and 70**
Students make a book of promises filled with examples of people who have kept promises.

**The Frog Prince
Puppets ....pages 71 and 72**
Students use a prop-up well and stick puppets to retell the story of the frog and the princess. Have student store the puppets in the well before putting the set into the pocket.

The Frog Prince

Story characters:

 Frog

 Princess

 King

 Prince

I liked this story:

☐ Yes

☐ No

This bookmark belongs to

_____

(your name)

Share The Frog Prince

Preview the Story

State the title of the story, and have students read aloud the names of the characters listed on the bookmark. Distribute copies of the story (pages 64 and 65), and have students preview the pictures. Invite students who are unfamiliar with the story to predict what happens to the frog.

Read the Story

Read the story aloud as students follow along. Encourage students to track the text and underline or frame key words. List and discuss any unfamiliar words, such as *glowed*, *jewels*, *creature*, *pale*, and *fond*. Point out picture clues and context clues that help explain parts of the story. After you have read the story aloud, encourage students to reread the story independently or with a partner.

Review the Story

Discuss the characters, setting, and plot of the story. Ask questions such as the following to help students recall important details, identify cause-and-effect relationships, and share opinions:

- How did the ball end up in the well?
- What did the frog want from the princess?
- What did the princess do when the frog gave her the gold ball?
- How did the princess react when she found the frog eating off her plate?
- The king told the princess "a promise is a promise." What did that mean?
- What happened when the princess kissed the frog?
- What do you think the princess learned from this experience?

More to Explore

- Solve a Problem

  Have students recall how the princess got her ball out of the well. Ask them how she might have gotten the ball without the help of the frog. Invite students to share their problem-solving ideas.

- Irregular Past Tense Verbs

  List these present tense and past tense verbs on the chalkboard: *dive/dove*, *bring/ brought*, *throw/threw*, *take/took*, *fall/fell*, *think/thought*. Review the list with students. Explain that some past tense verbs do not end in *-ed*. Have students find sentences in the story that include the verbs listed on the board. Then invite them to share their own sentences.

- Compare and Contrast Different Versions

  Read aloud another version of "The Frog Prince." Work with students to compare and contrast the two versions, using a Venn diagram or a comparison chart.

The Frog Prince

The Frog Prince

Every day the princess played in the garden with her gold ball. It glowed as brightly as the sun. She loved it more than all the jewels in her crown.

One morning, the princess threw the gold ball over a tall tree and ran to catch it. Splash! It fell into a well.

The princess reached into the well for the ball, but the water was too deep. She cried because she couldn't think of anything else to do.

A frog hopped up beside her. "Why are you crying?" he asked.

"I lost my gold ball in the well. I can't reach it," answered the princess.

"I'll dive into the well and bring back the ball if you promise to take care of me," said the frog. "You must let me eat from your plate and take me wherever you go."

"I promise," said the princess.

 Literature Pockets—Folktales and Fairy Tales • EMC 2731

The frog dove into the well and brought back the ball. He gave the ball to the princess. As he was climbing out of the water, the princess left without even a thank you.

When the princess sat down at the dinner table that night, there was the frog. He was eating off her plate. "Get this creature away from me!" cried the princess.

"My dear," said the king, "this frog said that you promised to care for him. Is that true?"

"Yes, Father," answered the princess.

"A promise is a promise," said the king. "A princess keeps her word."

The princess took the frog with her everywhere. If she forgot him, he croaked so loudly everyone in the castle hurried to remind the princess, "A promise is a promise. A princess keeps her word."

One day the frog looked very pale. He couldn't even hop. "What's the matter?" she asked.

"Dear princess, I'm not well. I have one last wish."

The princess thought he was dying. By this time, she had grown very fond of the frog. "What is your wish?"

"One kiss," said the frog. "You won't be sorry."

The princess made a terrible face, then bent over and kissed the frog. As quick as a wink, the frog changed into a handsome prince. The frog prince and the princess were married and lived happily ever after.

Literature Pockets—Folktales and Fairy Tales • EMC 2731

A Crafty Frog Prince

Materials

- page 68, reproduced for each pair of students
- green construction paper needed for each frog:
  one 6" x 9" (15 x 23 cm) piece of paper—body
  two 1½" x 6" (4 x 15 cm) pieces of paper—arms
  two 1½" x 9" (4 x 23 cm) pieces of paper—legs
  six 2" x 3" (5 x 7.5 cm) pieces of paper—tops
  of legs, feet, eyes
- other construction paper needed for each frog:
  two 1½" x 2" (4 x 5 cm) pieces of white construction paper—eyes
  one 6" (15 cm) narrow strip of pink construction paper—tongue
  one 4" square (10 cm) of yellow construction paper—ball
- scissors
- glue
- black marking pen

Steps to Follow

❶ Guide students through the following steps to make a paper frog:

a. Cut out the body and eye parts as shown. Glue the white part of the eye inside the green part and draw a black pupil. Glue the eyes to the top of the body.

b. Finish the face. Draw a mouth with a black marking pen. Curl the pink paper on a pencil and then glue the curled paper to the corner of the mouth to make a tongue.

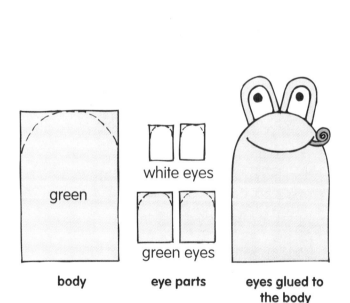

green

white eyes

green eyes

body   eye parts   eyes glued to
                                  the body

The Frog Prince

c. Cut out the arms and the gold ball as shown. Glue the arms to the back of the body and wrap them around to the front. Glue the hands on top of the ball to show the frog holding it.

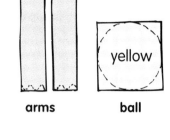

arms   ball

d. Accordion-fold the legs, folding each piece in half three times and then unfolding it and refolding back and forth accordion style. Glue the legs to the bottom of the body.

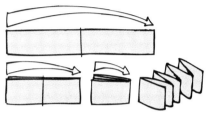

accordion-folded legs

e. Cut out the tops of the legs and the webbed feet as shown. Glue the tops of the legs to the bottom corners of the body, just above the folded strips. Glue the webbed feet to the bottoms of the folded strips. The frog is finished! You can fold him at his "waist" to make him sit up.

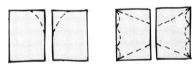

tops of the legs   webbed feet

❷ Ask students to imagine that they are the frog prince. Have them write on the form what the frog might say about the princess. Have them glue the completed form onto the back of the paper frog.

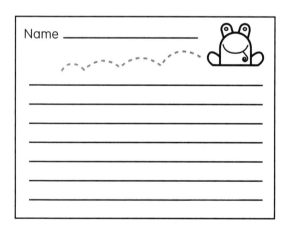

Name _____

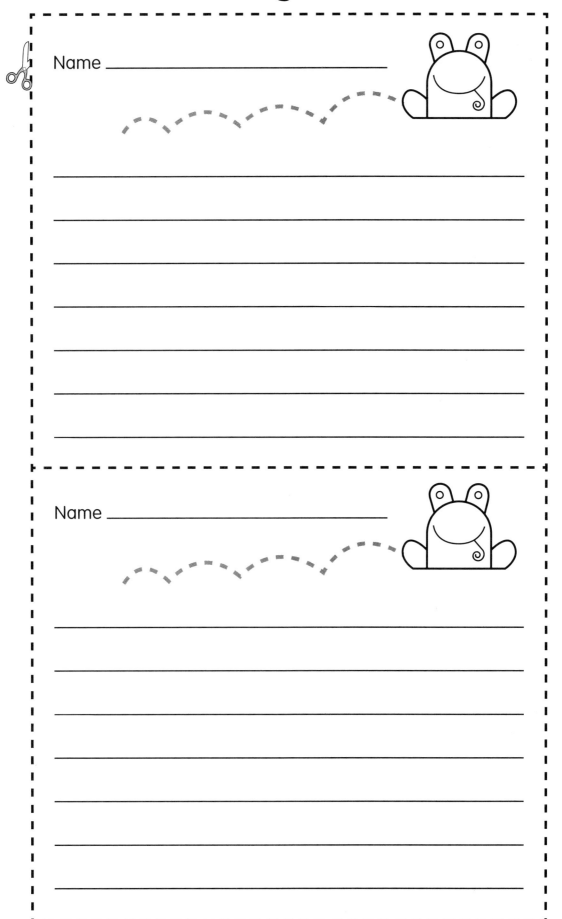

Name _____

_____

_____

_____

_____

_____

_____

Name _____

_____

_____

_____

_____

_____

_____

A Promise Is a Promise

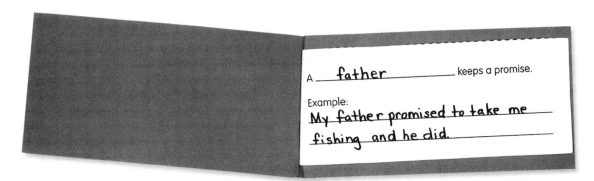

Materials

- page 70, reproduced for each student
- scissors
- 3" x 12" (7.5 x 30.5 cm) construction paper
- stapler

Steps to Follow

❶ Ask students to recall the promise made by the princess to the frog. Discuss how difficult it was for her to keep the promise. Then ask students to think of a promise they have made and how they kept that promise. Invite volunteers to share their experiences.

❷ List the following people on the chalkboard. Invite volunteers to say a promise that each person might make. Then have students brainstorm a list of other people and the promises they might make. Write their suggestions on the board.

firefighter	parent	friend
police officer	teacher	the president

❸ Distribute the Book of Promises sheet. Ask students to select three people from the list (or other people that they know) and write about those people on the sheet. For each section, students should write the person's name or occupation on the first line and then give an example of a promise the person would keep.

> A ___firefighter___ keeps a promise.
>
> Example:
>
> Firefighters promise to put out
>
> fires and they do.

❹ Have students cut apart the three sections (minibook pages) and the title strip of their Book of Promises. Have them make a cover by folding the construction paper in half and gluing the title onto the front. Have them put the three pages inside the cover and staple the book together on the left-hand side.

A Promise Is a Promise

by _____

A _____ keeps a promise.

Example:

_____

_____

A _____ keeps a promise.

Example:

_____

_____

A _____ keeps a promise.

Example:

_____

_____

A Book of Promises

The Frog Prince Puppets

Materials

- page 72, reproduced for each student
- 6" x 9" (15 x 23 cm) brown construction paper
- 8" x 9" (20 x 23 cm) yellow construction paper
- plastic straws
- glue
- black crayons or marking pens
- 5" x 8" (13 x 20 cm) index cards
- large craft sticks
- 2 paper clips

Steps to Follow

❶ Guide students through the following steps to make stick puppets and a paper well:

a. Fold the small construction paper in half to make the bottom of the well. Open the paper and glue two straws along the outer edge as shown. Close the paper, press along the edges, and let it dry. (The top of the well should be left unsealed.)

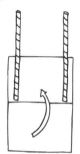

b. Fold the large construction paper in half and cut it as shown to make the top of the well. Open the paper and glue the other end of each straw in place. Close the paper, press down to seal it, and let it dry.

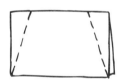

c. While the well is drying, color and cut out the characters. Glue them onto craft sticks. Glue the frog and the prince back to back on one stick.

d. After the well is dry, add details with a black crayon or marking pen. Make a removable prop-up stand by folding an index card as shown. Paper-clip the stand to the back of the well and adjust it as needed.

❷ Invite students to use their well and puppets to retell the story. When they finish, have them store the puppets in the well and then put the well into the pocket.

Note: Flatten the prop-up stand to fit the well into the pocket.

Puppet Patterns

The Emperor's New Clothes

Pocket Label and Bookmark .... page 74

Have students use these reproducibles to make The Emperor's New Clothes pocket label and bookmark. (See page 2.)

The Story of The Emperor's New Clothes .... pages 75–77

Share and discuss this story of an emperor who is fooled by two deceitful weavers. Reproduce the story on pages 76 and 77 for students. Use the teaching ideas on page 75 to preview, read, and review the story. Follow up with the "More to Explore" activities.

Weave a Cloak for the Emperor .... pages 78–80

Students create their own woven cloak for the emperor.

What Did They Say? .... pages 81 and 82

Students cut and paste dialog into speech bubbles to show what each character said in the story. Extend the activity by having students role-play or write a mock interview between a reporter and the characters.

The Emperor's New Clothes

Story characters:

 Emperor

 Weavers

 Advisor

 Townspeople

 Child

I liked this story:

☐ Yes

☐ No

This bookmark belongs to

_____

(your name)

Share The Emperor's New Clothes

Preview the Story
State the title of the story, and have students read aloud the names of the characters listed on the bookmark. Distribute copies of the story (pages 76 and 77), and have students preview the pictures. Invite students who are unfamiliar with the story to predict what the emperor discovers about his new clothes.

Read the Story
Read the story aloud as students follow along. Encourage students to track the text and underline or frame key words. List and discuss any unfamiliar words, such as *emperor, outfit, weaver, advisor, unfit,* and *style.* Point out picture clues and context clues that help explain parts of the story. After you have read the story aloud, encourage students to reread the story independently or with a partner.

Review the Story
Discuss the characters, setting, and plot of the story. Ask questions such as the following to help students recall important details, draw conclusions, and share opinions:

- What did the weavers promise the emperor?
- Why do you think the emperor believed the weavers could make magic cloth?
- What did the emperor give the weavers to make the cloth?
- What did the weavers do with the silk, gold thread, and jewels? Why?
- Why did everyone pretend that they could see the emperor's new clothes?
- What did the little boy say when he saw the emperor?
- What did the emperor do when he realized he wasn't wearing anything but underpants?

More to Explore

- Fit for the Job

  Discuss what being "fit for the job" means. Provide examples by listing the qualifications that would make an emperor fit for his job. Then divide the class into small groups. Have each group select a job and work together to make a list of qualifications that would make someone fit for that job. Then invite each group to read aloud their list to the class.

- Give Advice

  Discuss the role of an advisor. Have students consider what advice the advisor in the story might have given to the emperor. Then ask students what advice they would give if they were an advisor for an emperor, a king, or the president of the United States. Have them share their ideas aloud or in their journals.

- Compare and Contrast Different Versions

  Read aloud another version of "The Emperor's New Clothes." Work with students to compare and contrast the two versions, using a Venn diagram or a comparison chart.

The Emperor's New Clothes

Long ago there was an emperor who loved clothes. He wore as many new outfits in a day as he could.

One day two weavers came to the palace. "We weave the most beautiful cloth in the world," said the first weaver to the emperor. "Not only is the cloth beautiful, it is magic. Only people who are fit for their jobs can see the cloth."

"If you let us weave for you, we will make the finest outfit you have ever worn," said the second weaver. "And when you wear it, you will know which people in your kingdom are not fit for their jobs."

"Begin at once," said the emperor. "You must finish the new outfit before my grand parade."

The weavers set up a loom. They called for silk, gold thread, and jewels. They hid the treasures and pretended to weave all day.

After a few days, the emperor sent his advisor to see the cloth. The advisor saw nothing because there was nothing to see. He didn't tell the emperor. He thought he must be unfit for his job. Every day he talked about the beautiful cloth the weavers were making.

The Emperor's
New Clothes

The weavers pretended to work for many days. Finally they called for the emperor to tell him the outfit was ready. "Splendid," said the emperor. "It's done just in time for the grand parade."

The weavers pretended to dress the emperor. Then they took him to a large mirror. "Do you see how handsome you are?" they said.

The emperor couldn't see his new clothes. "I must be unfit for my job," he thought. "No one must know."

"It's magnificent!" the emperor said as he gave the weavers a bag of gold.

The emperor led the parade through town. People couldn't see the emperor's clothes, but they didn't want their neighbors to think they were unfit for their jobs. They told each other how handsome the emperor looked.

Suddenly a little boy shouted, "Look! The emperor isn't wearing anything but his underpants!"

The emperor knew that the boy spoke the truth. No child could be unfit for his job. He reached down and patted the boy on the head.

The emperor said, "It's a new style." He held his head high and went on with the parade.

Weave a Cloak for the Emperor

Materials

- page 80, reproduced
  for each student
- construction paper needed for each cloak:
  two 7" x 12" (18 x 30.5 cm) sheets of purple paper—cloak frame
  one 9" x 12" (23 x 30.5 cm) sheet of white or tan paper—body parts
- weaving strips needed for each cloak (include different kinds and
  colors of paper):
  five 1" x 12" (2.5 x 30.5 cm) strips of paper
  nine 1" x 7" (2.5 x 18 cm) strips of paper
  three or four 7" (18 cm) strands of gold giftwrap ribbon (thin)
- glue
- scissors
- crayons or marking pens

Steps to Follow

❶ Remind students that the emperor was left without new clothes. Tell them that their job will be to weave a new cloak for the emperor to wear.

❷ Guide students through the following steps to make the cloak. Demonstrate each step:

a. Select five of the long paper strips and nine of the short paper strips in a variety of colors. Also take three or four strands of the gold ribbon to weave into the cloak.

b. Start by laying one sheet of the purple construction paper vertically on the table. Lay the five long paper strips vertically on top, side by side, leaving a border of space along the outer sides of the purple paper. Glue down the top end of each strip.

c. Weave each short strip through the long strips to create a pattern. Weave the first strip over-under-over-under-over; weave the second strip under-over-under-over-under, and so on. After you weave each strip, glue down the ends to secure the strip in place. At some point, weave the gold ribbons into the pattern. After you weave all the strips, glue down the bottom ends of the long strips.

d. Mark a 1½" (4 cm) border around the outside edge of the second sheet of purple paper. Cut on this line to make a frame (a border with the middle cut out).

e. Place the frame over the woven paper and glue it in place. Round the top corners to make the emperor's shoulders.

f. Color and cut out the parts of the emperor and glue them onto white or tan construction paper. Then cut out the pieces again. Glue them onto the cloak to complete the emperor as shown.

❸ Display the emperors for everyone to see. Invite students to compare and contrast the cloaks. When the display comes down, store the emperors in students' pockets.

Body Patterns

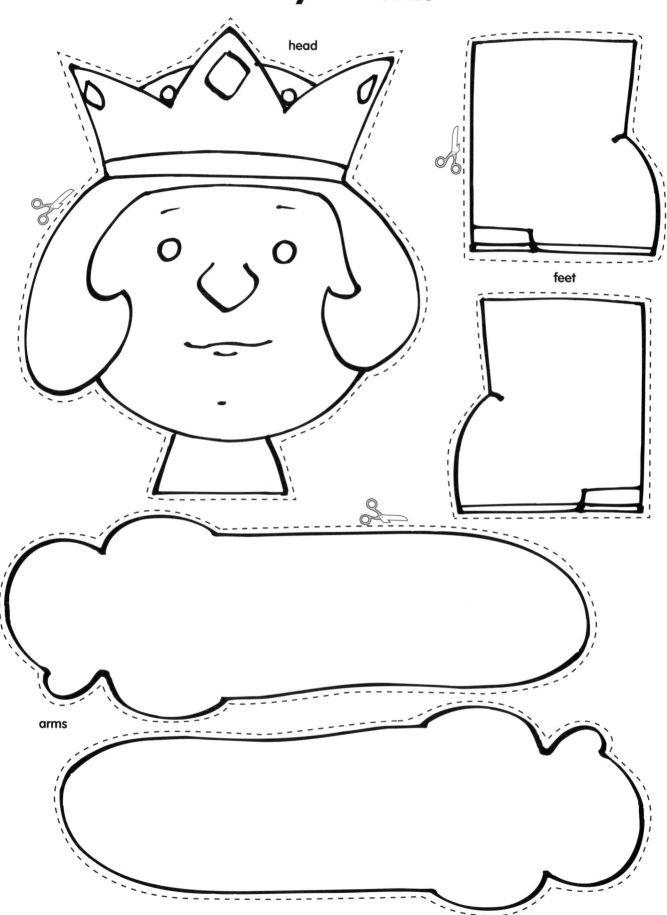

head

feet

arms

80

Note: Reproduce pages 81 and 82 for each student. Use the directions given on page 73 to help students complete the activity.

Name: _____

What Did They Say?

Speech Bubbles

Look! The emperor isn't wearing anything but his underpants!

The cloth the weavers are making is beautiful.

It's a new style.

We weave the most beautiful cloth in the world.

Look how handsome the emperor looks!

Literature Pockets—Folktales and Fairy Tales • EMC 2731

The Bremen Town Musicians

Pocket Label and Bookmark ....page 84

Have students use these reproducibles to make The Bremen Town Musicians pocket label and bookmark. (See page 2.)

The Story of The Bremen Town Musicians .... pages 85–87

Share and discuss this story of four old animals who scare off a band of thieves. Reproduce the story on pages 86 and 87 for students. Use the teaching ideas on page 85 to preview, read, and review the story. Follow up with the "More to Explore" activities.

Animal Totem .... pages 88–90

Students follow step-by-step directions to create a two-medium picture of the four animals one on top of the other as described in the story.

Write a Song................... pages 91 and 92

Here's an opportunity for students to create a song for the animals to sing on their way to town to be street musicians.

Make a Guitar .... pages 93 and 94

Students create rubber-band guitars to pluck as they sing their animal songs.

The Bremen Town Musicians

Story characters:

 Donkey

 Dog

 Cat

 Rooster

 Thieves

I liked this story:

☐ Yes

☐ No

This bookmark belongs to

_____
(your name)

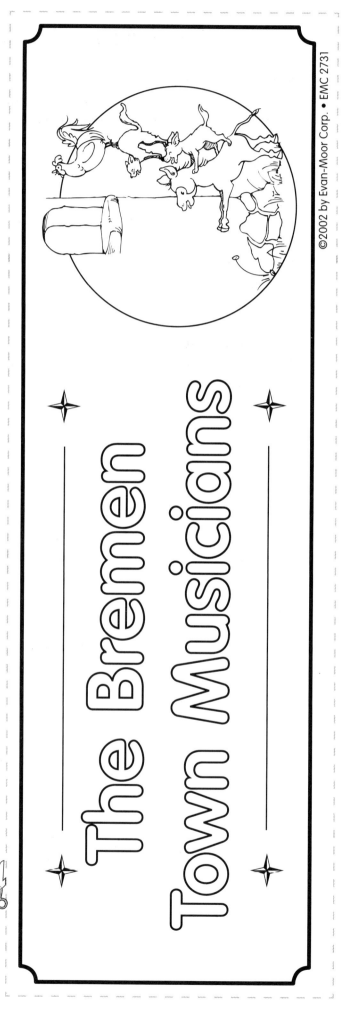

Share The Bremen Town Musicians

Preview the Story

State the title of the story, and have students read aloud the names of the characters listed on the bookmark. Distribute copies of the story (pages 86 and 87), and have students preview the pictures. Invite students who are unfamiliar with the story to predict how a donkey, dog, cat, and rooster scare off some thieves.

Read the Story

Read the story aloud as students follow along. Encourage students to track the text and underline or frame key words. List and discuss any unfamiliar words, such as *grain*, *mill*, *loads*, *musician*, *brayed*, and *mistress*. Point out picture clues and context clues that help explain parts of the story. After you have read the story aloud, encourage students to reread the story independently or with a partner.

Review the Story

Discuss the characters, setting, and plot of the story. Ask questions such as the following to help students recall the sequence of events, identify important details, and draw conclusions:

- Who did the donkey meet first? Next? Last?
- Why did the animals leave their homes?
- Why did the animals look into the window of the house?
- How did they know the men were thieves?
- What frightened the thieves?
- Why did one of the thieves come back to the house?
- How did the animals scare him off?

More to Explore

- Animal Jobs

  Ask students to recall the jobs that the animals had in the story. Then work with students to brainstorm a list of other animal jobs. Have students consider animals that help at farms, animals that transport people or things throughout the world, and animals that help people with special needs.

- Animal Sounds

  Work with students to brainstorm a list of animals in alphabetical order. Discuss which animals make sounds that we can hear. Write the sound words next to those animals. Then invite students to make those sounds.

- Compare and Contrast Different Versions

  Read aloud another version of "The Bremen Town Musicians." Work with students to compare and contrast the two versions, using a Venn diagram or a comparison chart.

The Bremen Town Musicians

Every day a donkey took grain to the mill. He was getting old and couldn't carry heavy loads anymore. One morning he heard his master say, "I'm going to get rid of that donkey."

This frightened the donkey, so he ran away. "I'll be a street musician," he thought. "I sing very well."

The donkey saw a dog by the road. "What's wrong?" brayed the donkey.

"My master said I am too old to hunt. He won't give me food, so I ran away."

"Come with me," said the donkey. "We'll be street musicians and sing for our supper."

The dog followed the donkey. Soon they met a cat. "Cat, what's wrong?" brayed the donkey.

"I am too old. I can't catch mice, so my mistress is going to drown me."

"Come with us," brayed the donkey. "We'll all be street musicians."

The dog followed the donkey. The cat followed the dog. Along the way they saw a rooster.

"Oh, woe is me," crowed the rooster.

"Rooster, what is wrong?" brayed the donkey.

"I am too old. The farmer told the cook to put me in a stew."

"You sing very well," said the donkey. "Come with us. We'll all be street musicians."

The dog followed the donkey. The cat followed the dog. The rooster followed the cat. The four animals walked through the forest. They came to a house and stood one on top of the other so the rooster could see in the window. "There are three men eating dinner," said the rooster. "They must be thieves. There are bags of coins on the table."

"It makes no difference who they are. We're hungry. We'll sing for our supper," brayed the donkey. The animals brayed, barked, meowed, and crowed.

"Listen to that noise. The army has come to get us," said one of the thieves. The men ran into the woods, and the animals ate their food. After dinner the animals blew out the candles and went to sleep.

One of the men came back to get the money. He lit a candle. The cat's eyes glowed in the light, and she scratched the man's face. When he ran out the door, the dog bit him, the donkey kicked him, and the rooster crowed loudly.

The man ran to the other thieves. "Monsters!" he yelled. The thieves ran away and never came back.

The four old animals stayed in their new home. They lived there happily the rest of their lives.

Animal Totem

Materials

- pages 89 and 90, reproduced for each student
- newspapers
- midnight blue or black tempera wash (paint mixed with water)
- paintbrushes
- 6" x 12" (15 x 30.5 cm) white drawing paper
- crayons
- tape (optional)

Steps to Follow

❶ Set up paint stations. Cover the worktables with newspaper. Set out the tempera wash and paintbrushes.

❷ Have students use crayons and the directions on pages 89 and 90 to draw the four animals standing on top of one another. Students should stack the animals from largest to smallest, with the rooster on top. Tell them to draw stars for the background. Remind students to draw heavily so the images will appear when the tempera wash is painted over the picture.

❸ Have students paint the tempera wash over the entire paper to create the nighttime sky.

❹ Extend the activity by having students write about the animals' experiences. Students may write a paragraph or a newspaper article about what happened. Distribute writing paper that has been trimmed to match the size of the picture. Have students tape the written description onto the back of the dried picture.

Donkey and Dog Drawing Steps

Donkey

Dog

Cat and Rooster Drawing Steps

Cat

Rooster

Write a Song

Materials

- page 92, reproduced for each student
- 9" x 12" (23 x 30.5 cm) construction paper
- crayons
- glue

Steps to Follow

❶ Review with students the main characters of the story. Have students produce the sound each animal might make as it brays, barks, meows, or crows. Then explain to students that they are going to complete a song for the animals to sing as they walk toward town.

❷ Distribute the song sheets and read the incomplete lyrics with students. Point out the repeating pattern. Ask students to identify the parts that change in each verse.

❸ Have students work as a class, with a partner, or independently to complete the final two verses of the song. Then have them color the pictures and glue the finished song sheet onto construction paper.

❹ Have more advanced students write their own original song based on what happened in the story.

❺ After students finish writing the song, have them come up with a simple tune for it. Students may use the guitar they make in the next activity (see pages 93 and 94) to pluck the tune as they sing their song to the class.

The Bremen Town Musicians

Name: _____

My Song

Hee-haw, hee-haw,

Listen to my song.

Hee-haw, hee-haw,

Why don't you come along?

Hee-haw, bow-wow,

Listen to our song.

Hee-haw, bow-wow,

Why don't you come along?

Hee-haw, bow-wow, _____,

Listen to our song.

Hee-haw, bow-wow, _____,

Why don't you come along?

Hee-haw, bow-wow,

_____, _____,

Listen to our song.

Hee-haw, bow-wow,

_____, _____,

Why don't you come along?

Make a Guitar

Materials

- page 94, reproduced for each student
- 1" x 1½" (2.5 x 4 cm) pieces of cardboard
- paint stirrers or wooden rulers
- tagboard file folders, cut in half
- rubber bands
- scissors
- crayons
- glue

cardboard bridge

Steps to Follow

❶ Guide students through the following steps to make a rubber-band guitar:

a. Glue three 1" x 1½" pieces of cardboard together to make the guitar's bridge. Glue the bridge to the wooden piece, about 3" (7.5 cm) from one end. Allow this part to dry completely.

b. Cut out the guitar template. Lay it on tagboard and trace around it. Cut out the guitar shape. Use crayons to add details to the guitar.

c. Stretch two rubber bands lengthwise around the wooden piece. Be sure they go over the bridge. Note: If you have a rambunctious class, lay some ground rules for proper use of rubber bands before passing them out.

d. Glue the wooden piece to the tagboard and let the guitar dry completely.

❷ Invite students to pluck their guitars as they sing their song about the Bremen Town musicians. (See the previous activity.)

Variation

Invite students to construct a more sophisticated guitar using a variety of thick and thin rubber bands and a movable bridge. Encourage them to create a variety of tones with their guitars.

The Bremen
Town Musicians

Guitar Pattern

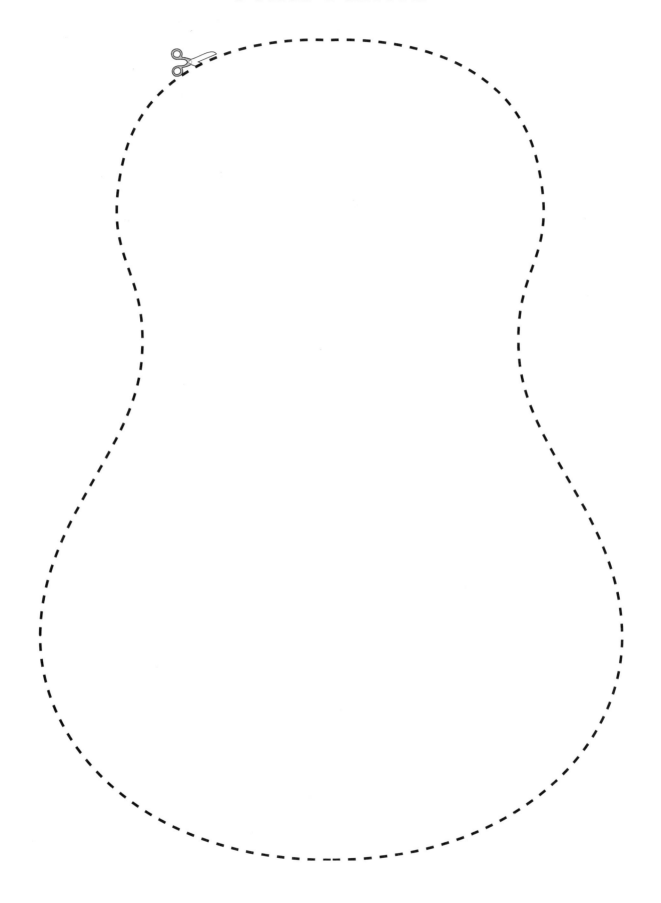

Literature Pockets—Folktales and Fairy Tales • EMC 2731

Folktales and Fairy Tales

My favorite folktale/fairy tale is _____

I like it best for these three reasons:

1. _____

2. _____

3. _____

Draw your favorite character here.

List words that describe your favorite character.

_____

_____

_____

_____

Folktales and Fairy Tales

Fill in the circle in front of each thing you could find in a folktale or fairy tale. If you fill in the circle, give an example from a folktale or fairy tale.

○ talking animals

_____

○ giants, trolls, or elves

_____

○ a spaceship on the moon

_____

○ a magical character or event

_____

○ a trip to the mall

_____

○ nonliving things that talk

_____

○ old-fashioned clothes and buildings

_____

○ computers, televisions, or cell phones

_____